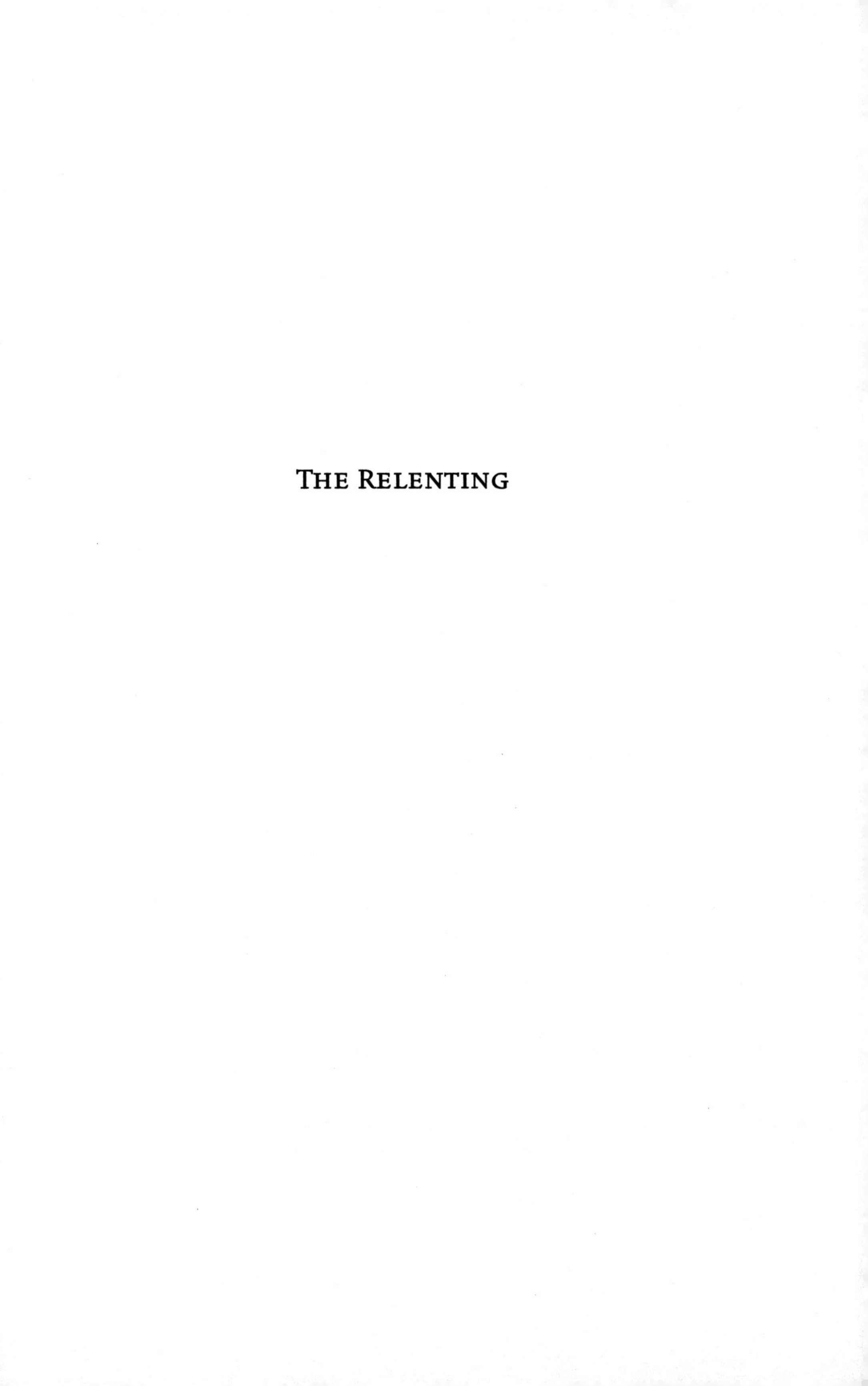

THE RELENTING

The Relenting

A Play of Sorts

Lisa Gill

New Rivers Press :: Minnesota

First Edition
Library of Congress Control Number: 2010923063
ISBN: 978-0-89823-254-7

Cover Painting by Travis J. Farnsworth
("Goddess," / detail, 9 inches x 12 inches, acrylic on canvas, private collection).
Artist contact: tjf__282@hotmail.com

Book Design by JB Bryan/La Alameda Press
Set in Vendetta with titling in Golden

Publication of this book made possible by a Gratitude Award
from New Mexico Literary Arts, the McKnight Foundation,
and other contributors to New Rivers Press.

New Rivers Press is a nonprofit literary press associated
with Minnesota State University Moorhead.

New Rivers Press
MSUM
1104 7th Avenue South
Moorhead, MN 56563
www.newriverspress.com

Printed in the United States of America

For

women

who

confront

real

or

metaphorical

rattlers

with

grace.

Contents

Look like the innocent flower
But be the serpent under it
—WILLIAM SHAKESPEARE

We must combine the toughness of the serpent
with the softness of the dove,
a tough mind and a tender heart
—MARTIN LUTHER KING, JR.

The Catalyst & the Evolution

"The Relenting" began at dusk on September 29, 2009, when I found a rattlesnake coiled on the brick floor of my living room in my cabin outside Moriarty, New Mexico. What's a two hour stand-off with a rattlesnake if not a primal encounter waiting to be interpreted?

Ecdysis is the word for the skin sloughing snakes do and might as well be the word for the process writers go through with revisions of certain manuscripts, those texts whose life cycles demand we shed draft after draft, abandoning each accrued preconception to ultimately access deeper instinct.

Creativity always requires metamorphosis. Think Ovid. The initial encounter with the rattlesnake transformed first into an email sent to seven friends, then manifested as insomnia wracked with echoes of rattling. The insomnia provoked days of checking behind the bookcase; that checking led to journal entries; those notes turned into an essay that grew into a lyric memoir before transforming into a sequence of prose poems; the prose poems ended up necessitating line breaks before being scripted for two voices; the scripted poems mandated more dialogue... until the words became a play staged so deep in the heart of archetype that final work becomes for me—night after night—nothing but a dream.

The process meant everything. As with the skins that snakes shed, the texts left behind held the imprint of the scale patterns of the full grown work, as identifiable as the snake skin left beneath my lilac bush, as distinctive as the wanton joy that snake must have felt when freed from a constricting text.

What's funny is that I knew, from the first, what the text needed: long lines, both high and low diction, complex syntax, and multiple languages. (Originally I intended a minimum of six; three, besides English, remain.) My ear was at play early, since the moment the snake first rattled at me.

And so was my eye. At one point, kneeling on a wooden rocker a couple feet from the rattler, I tried to gauge his length by following the coils with an imaginary seamstress's tape; I erred on the short side. Afterwards, during the writing, my eye still demanded to be sated. I gathered images from archeological texts and art books, anything depicting a woman and a snake. One stood out, the goddess now reinterpreted on the cover by Travis J. Farnsworth. For months I kept on the front of my notebook a photograph of the Minoan Snake Goddess, a sculpture first found in the temple repositories in the palace at Knossos, Crete. All I knew right then was that I wanted—at least once in the writing—to feel like her, to have reason to lift my arms skyward, to hold both the real and the metaphorical snake with both command and empathy and to do so with enough grace to keep a cat balanced on the top my head. Really, I wanted to pray like that.

And I needed to pray. For a month following the snake encounter, I was plagued with traumatic flashbacks from my past, a veritable ungodly procession of the things I don't usually like to envision. But I was no longer alone. The snake was my guide, a catalyst for a much needed shifting of the meaning of those flashbacks. I discovered I understood more about my own history than I did prior to meeting the rattler.

What I knew was less fear and more gratitude.

And with gratitude came the hunger for knowledge, for understanding, for empathy. I pored over research until I could develop an intellectual intimacy. And when I did find a pronounced empathy with both the capacity for venom and the simultaneous vulnerability of the snake, that's when I came back around to the Minoan Snake Goddess. That's when I reached the word "communion." And that's when the writing was complete.

The Characters

WOMAN: The woman has a few traits that matter: poetic disposition and a gift for both seriousness and humor. She is in her thirties, unmarried, and significantly unpartnered with a history of rape, incest, and domestic violence—but more importantly there is also a history of fending off attempted assaults, a pronounced resilience and emotional fluency with surviving against odds. She is able-bodied but recently out of a wheelchair so at least conscious of physical vulnerability. The personal history is weighty, but is matched by the capacity for joy, openness to learning and receptivity. The encounter with the snake sheers all her stories off the bones of the present and reduces her to bare essentials of moment-by-moment mindfulness; the past is visibly shed in the interaction and desire awakens.

SNAKE: The snake is androgynous but can be assumed male because of the woman's history and limitations of interpreting the sex of a predator and because of archetype. He represents raw instinct and appetite with a capacity for natural wisdom and a far greater level of tolerance and self-acceptance and environmental hardiness than humans. He is a creature of great sensuality, occasionally lewd and/or crude without understanding the full ramifications of words in the context of the woman's life. A seer with a natural vision that transcends the limitations of being human, he is physically seductive, flirtatious, a combination of swift and still, infinitely patient without sacrificing any realism. The snake becomes alternately predator, mentor, cohort, lover—and assumes the archetypal significance of teaching the woman to accept the absurdity of her own fate and learn to find beauty therein.

Unseen Characters:

Cognitive Behavioral Therapist (spoken to on phone)
Sheriff's Deputy (speculated about)

The Setting

Literal: The entire play takes place in the woman's living room. Picture a brick floor, old woodstove, rocker, lots of bookshelves. As important as the internal setting, which the woman refers to as a heart, is the external setting where the play is not happening, the environment around the house, the landscape that houses the snake, the natural world illuminated in some detail in Act One. None of the literal setting needs to be replicated on the stage except for one tall backed chair and one ottoman.

Symbolic: The play is set in the left ventricle of the human heart, which represents everything heart symbolism automatically conjures as well as the literal geographic reference within the two sides and four chambers of her cabin. The set should be a cross between house and physical body, and must at times, due to lighting cues, resemble a chamber reached deep under the earth as part of an archetypal descent. The door, which was literally closed until the woman used a cane from her collection to push it open, is here symbolized as the mitral valve that leads from the heart back into the larger archetypal body of the world we all share. The mitral valve should also hint at birth canal.

:: Act One ::
REVELATION

(This short act introduces both characters in full regalia so the archetypal journey can begin. The woman will emerge from within the audience, wearing blue jeans, camisole, and no shoes. The snake begins seated in the high backed chair, which faces the back of the stage, with only his head and neck visible poking around the side of the chair. The snake is costumed elaborately as a diamondback, including eye make-up that showcases large vertical fixed pupils that are visible when eyes are closed—and arched brows.)

WOMAN

(Woman begins a slow approach towards snake.)

I am barefoot, bluejeans, cotton camisole when we meet.
Your eyes steady on mine, vertical pupils,
and for a moment there is not panic. There is only recognition
of the environmental topography we are not at this moment sharing:

Not the rash of wildsprung asters
under the windmill;
Not the chasms of 4 o'clock blossoms
near the piñon;

Not the broken clothesline still noosed
in a high branch of the juniper;
Nor the sun-mashed berry-pulp beneath.

No gopher holes;
No orb weaver's web suspended
from the eave;
None of the ever-mythic maws
that are the gaping black-toothed yucca pods.

Not even grass blades proliferating
and wind-whipped;
Or the old tire discarded by the gate;
The older barn
at the side of the property.

No back gate; no front gate; no exits.

Where are the rocks and boulders? The crevices in between?
Where are the chunks of broken concrete that line my driveway?
Where is the earth under my feet?
Where is the dirt?

Am I still standing naked ankles and toes on ruddy basketweave?
Is the pattern underfoot the one I bricked on top of a bare concrete slab
to hold the sun in the floor of my living room all winter long?
Is this the sun?

I am barefoot, blue jeans, caught up in the idea that something about
this is wrong.

This much I know:

The sun, yes, is here but about to set, and I am still standing
naked feet and ankles and toes, naked collarbone and arms,
—not even a bra—
I am standing still and I am looking at you.

Or rather, I am looking at your neck,
and you have one,
narrow, smooth slope, lightly tanned.
Between the width of your jaw and the girth of your body
come such tender concave lines that yes, I do,
I know who you are:
rattler.

(Woman steps farther back and snake stands up for full reveal, turning to face the back of stage, pausing, and then turning back to face audience again.)

SNAKE

(Snake is still standing but moves farther to stage left so that Woman and Snake are equally spread across the stage.)

You are barefoot bluejeans caught up in the idea
that something about this is wrong, that something
about this is song. What's wrong? What's song?
Dear, you will go deaf.
You will swim in deep adrenaline,
dark waters of visceral fear.

Already your pulse quickens, your breath
sharp as any misunderstanding, already your body
a statue in some park, safe un-chafed landing
for a lark with an olive branch in its beak.

Still you are weak.

You are barefoot bluejeans caught up in the idea
that something about this is wrong.

Only this:
You are not undressed for our encounter.

(*Woman removes jeans and camisole to uncover long diamondback dress.*)

You are longing.

You are not dressed for our encounter.

(*Woman adds stockings with garters and tall black high-heeled boots.*)

You are longing.

Let there be appropriate adornment of the body...

(*Woman accepts necklace—at arm's length and without touching fingers—
from Snake, attaches it, poses for full reveal and turns around full circle.*)

:: Act Two ::
INTERSPECIES ALTERCATION

(This act is the body of the play and encompasses the entire journey the snake and woman take together, aside from recognition and release. It requires tight physical compression and hearty magnetism. It also requires fierce resistance to touch that gradually is eroded by the development of trust, which leads ultimately to magnetism and repulsion, dance of a dialogue and a brutal embrace. At no point should the snake and woman be more than three and a half feet apart—although close synchronized or stalking movements may take the duo all around the stage. Much of their interaction depends on mirroring and so consciousness should be paid to physical and spacial gestures, rises and falls, and the use of the two pieces of furniture, the tall wing-backed green chair and the ottoman. The entire compressed stage will be fully utilized, and during the course of this act, even the wing-backed chair will face all four directions.)

WOMAN

I am longing.
My house is a heart.
A small thing beating in Deer Valley.
A gift from my mother.
Two large conjoined rooms with two subchambers.

SNAKE

Ventricle atrium ventricle atrium.
Blood coursing the way of replenishment and restoration.

WOMAN

Compassionate quiet on 3.6 fenced acres under the Milky Way.

SNAKE

The silky way. The night-sky heat-sniffing hunting way.
Nocturnal, knocked down into the dirt eternal, I am fear infernal.

WOMAN

This is a solitary place, deep inside my body
and yet you sit in the left ventricle
    as if you were meant to be here,
    as if you know what it means to be close to me
        or know the way into my body,
    as if we were already intimate.

SNAKE

Contentment is a biological trait, an undeniable fate.
Cohabitation is possible.
Even here is an opportunity: I can eat the mice in your house.
Mmmmm, gulp.

WOMAN

Genus Crotalus, how did we get here?
To this place where we have selected each other?
As if companionship were natural and not hatched
from some toothed plan to fit our bodies into the innate order
by any means possible?

SNAKE

Get here? Get lost. Be found. We are here.
Here is where we are and here is where we will be.

WOMAN

I wish this moment were simpler than a woman trying to negotiate
with a snake.

Desert Carnivore, I'd love to give you an excuse
that would pass in school or for a missed lunchdate.
Yet, I already know better—**I have always known better.**
When don't justifications pale or do some grand disservice to
something
that could be as honest as acknowledging divergent priorities
or accepting an everyday failure?

Here in my living room, my sad and mundane story merits no regard:
disabled woman who just a few months back got out of
a wheelchair;

woman who's likely to need it again.
There is no place for pity.
You don't care whether or not today is a good walking day,
might prefer to bring me down,
encourage disease to disown my arms and legs,
leave me living torso.

Already you rib me,
your dexterous body nothing but internal spokes attached to a skull.

Am I any different, chest heaving?

(*Snake silent, gloating.*)

Have you no compassion?

(*Snake silent, ponderous.*)

What are you thinking? Now, this moment, here, where we are.

(*Snake silent, meditating.*)

Am I going to have to milk you to get anything more out of you?

SNAKE

(*Snake whispers.*)

Nay...

WOMAN

I could milk you,
make my hand a fistful of your neck,
thumb and forefinger at the hinge-pins of your jaws.

SNAKE

(*Snake whispers.*)

My nape.

WOMAN

I could pry your toothed mouth open as a sheet of paper,
thin-tongued label on the unmarked mason jar.

SNAKE

(*Snake whispers.*)

Glass scrape.

WOMAN

Your fangs would succumb,
rotate up from the roof of your mouth,
protrude over the glass lip:

SNAKE

(Snake whispers.)

Agape, me.

WOMAN

Two tubes of spurt,
nectar of hemotoxin and hearth—

I know how to handle you.

SNAKE

(Snake whispers, sinking down.)

Rape me.

WOMAN

What have you been mumbling about?
Escape thee? Drape me? Berate a tree?
You've got a bung knee?

(Snake silent, stewing.)

What do you want, Spiral Creeper, coming here into my house?

(Snake silent, stewing.)

Weren't we chatting up a storm a minute ago?
Back in Genesis?
Sharing an apple?
Didn't our little banter get me into a bit of trouble
and get you reviled?
I fell; you crawled.
Is that why you don't want to talk now?

(*Snake silent, stewing.*)

Give me something. A little more.
εν αρκη ην ο λογοσ
In the beginning was the word.
λογοσ, a word.
The word.
The life-giving word.
και ο λογοσ ην προσ τον θεον
And the word was toward the light.
Let there be language.

SNAKE

Affluent.
Continent.
Satin stitch.
God of war.

WOMAN

Affront?

Abhor. High pitch. Core.

SNAKE

Stunt. Score. Stitch. Or?

WOMAN

Hunt. Pour. Kitsch.

SNAKE

Cunt. Whore. Bitch.

(*Woman Sinking. Snake oblivious.*)

Cunt. Roar. Snitch.
Hunt. More. Bitch.
Bunt. Whore. Rich.

(*Woman Sunk.*)

Cunt. Whore. Bitch?

(*Snake bears witness becomes empathetic and apologetic, tries to be helpful.*)

Transform old sore . . .

(Snake begins to invite, even cajole—without touch—
the Woman to rise back up.)

Confront. Restore. Enrich.

WOMAN

Runt.
Floor.
Hitch?

(Woman stands up.)

SNAKE

Stunt.   Soar.   Niche.

WOMAN

Treasure hunt.
        Adore.
                Wild boar.
                        Bewitch.

SNAKE

Contentment.
                Country store.
Drainage Ditch.

WOMAN

Switch.

SNAKE

Pitch.

WOMAN

Snake Oil Doctor, deaf as you are, already you listen better than that
drunk human
who barely responded to the nonverbal communication
between my hand and his penis.

At twenty-nine my mouth runneth'd over with negations,
refutations, bargains, two-letter words in such close
juxtaposition
I cursed a shipyard into the desert.

Never has there existed a guarantee any human will know
the meaning of the word, "No."

So I said, **Let there be bone.**
And I put my hand under my skirt
until phalanges formed a barrier
in front of that chance opening
chromosomes created between my legs.

Bang bang bang that guy's prick
on the living chastity belt.

We abstained from the dynamic of rapist
        and rape victim
by sheer dint of his deficit.
My attention was greater than his.
My clasp of my own crotch infinite.

SNAKE

I am sorry.

WOMAN

No rhyme?

SNAKE

No.
I know rape.
I know rape of the land.
I know rape of the body.
I know kicked in the gut.
I know a boot in the face.
I know the jaw forced open,
mouth violenced with every unwanted.
I even know dropped from a hawk's claws.

WOMAN

I am sorry.

SNAKE

You and I also know resilience.
We know the gash; we know the gash closing.
We learn grace on par with every horror:
let go,
move on,
grow,
change,
recover,
Find flow—
the rhythm of wax and wane.

WOMAN

This is insane but I am glad you and I are on speaking terms

(Woman turns chair to face stage right, away from snake, but kneels there and peers over at snake.)

because I am not today a fan of reticence.
After sitting at two deathbeds in two months
where I crassly pried decorum open with a crowbar
and spilled all my gut-rendered unspokens publicly

—enough to make bystanders blush—
still I am not a fan of reticence. I can't be.

I am longing.

So now, here, in my house, I look at your body
currently so very properly restrained,
curled as if coiled in some shaman's basket before the lid is removed,
and I almost think you actually **want** to be well behaved, as if
—because you're a snake and can die peacefully in any environment—
you don't realize
the quilts on every death bed are knit from regret.

SNAKE

Seed stitch.
Rice stitch.
Unspoken purled ladder
that leads ultimately through sadness
to some kind of acceptance
of things being exactly what they need to be
in time.

WOMAN

I suppose so, yes.
Even reticence.
Reticence can be what it needs to be in time.

SNAKE

I am not today a fan of reticence.

Even your body, climbing the chair back
and staying out of my reach saddens me.
But I understand.
Any closer and I would bite you.

WOMAN

I could almost want that.

SNAKE

I don't. Nor do you.

WOMAN

You're right and you're wrong.
Perhaps we are both already conflicted.
Look how you let me pick you up with a line of Greek,
a yarn spun deep into story.
Look how you picked me up.
Even at this distance, we pit our lives one against the other:

SNAKE

Twin rib.

Triangle rib.
Two by two rib.

WOMAN

Two beings already knit so tight
the intertwining will stay with us forever,
leave us kinked and bent and curving
and intoning the muscle memory of each other
long after the unraveling and disentangling...

SNAKE

Yes.

WOMAN

Yes.

SNAKE

Yes.

WOMAN

I desire all of this because time is short
            —you and I have exactly forty-seven minutes together—
so what's terminal is my own agitation,
my flat impatience with this still dance.

Let this lead quickly to the inevitable religious rise
towards the heavens of hiss and spit and rattle against God,
the climax of every good hour spent loving life
and begrudging temperance,
shaking time by the shoulders
for another day,
or hour,
or ten minutes of looking into the
unfinished.

Because even here, in this stand-off, is the hunger for life, a thirst for trust.

SNAKE

There is no such thing as trust.

WOMAN

There is **less** distrust.

SNAKE

Ha. **You?**

WOMAN

I try. What about you?
Deeply camouflaged in scales that let you merge

with dirt,
with earth,
with the soft and hard landscape of invisibility.
Not even the hawk circling the sky can find you,
and then humans have to practically step on you
to elicit a rattle of your presence.

I'd like to see you go up against the world un-camouflaged,
more or less unhidden,
at least a little bit unguarded,
all your defenses scaled back
until you might be open as a book turned
to a single page where the tip of a woman's
finger
marks the place some random encounter
began...
because random works the alchemy of fate
and this encounter is no less valid
than any endeavor plotted for years.
Chance may be the only coveted clutch
of possibilities so fantastic
they haven't even been dreamed yet
and **I am longing:**
I want these new dreams...

do you?

SNAKE

I'm here, aren't I?

In my dreams, I take your hand
and hold it ever so gently

inside my mouth and no one screams.

because I can control my venom, wouldn't
—no way, never, no chance, no time, no place—
leave you maimed.
Or unhappy.
Or unpleased.

My entire body is ribbed!

I offer hundreds of curved bones
to round out your dozens.

See how quickly this experience of *me*
becomes systemic?
It's genetic memory, baby.
Past-life-current-love-fated.

Let there be—wink wink—the two of us sated.

WOMAN

You with your Two Penises, those Happy Hemipenes,...

SNAKE

Are you sure I'm male?

WOMAN

Sure enough
what's untouchable is desire:
thirty-six of Boticelli's curves in a museum piece roped off,
fragments of roundness that loop in the imagination of pure shape,
visceral wish to touch.

You are not snake, you are abstraction of circle.

I'm tempted; I'm taunted.

The alarm of your tail resounds already in speculation
and yet, look at you—
                                        peaceful coiled hush.
My mind stretches towards you,
inches around the maze of your spine,
and meters away from you,
recoiling,
my own body S-ing.

This apartness,
this knowledge of essential separation pains me plentiful.
Logic and sensuality ride the length of my spine,
twined together,
a braid of wish and wash:
I do not want to be punctured;
I do not want to puncture.

This barrier of physical distance,
a mere three and a half feet,
could be broached with a feather
from the dove that breaks morning
on the line outside the house.

Peace?
Stasis?
Fallible seduction?

I cannot frighten you. I will not.

SNAKE

We are in this together.
Sincerely.
What's yours is mine. Vice. Versa-
tile vices are ours to enjoy.
The world is our canvas to tag.
And chase.
And "Tag, you're it!"

One symbol, or a bit of spray-paint,
two hearts within the walls of one body,
we are in this together.

WOMAN

Snake and woman tied together with a hemp rope?
With a chain?
With a ball and chain?
Some anchor or a magician's handkerchief
or a belt
or a ring of legal obligations
          and American cultural hetero-normative sap and crap and
                    rapture
                    and regulation,
                                        a miscarriage of
                                   expectations,
as if either of us can assuage the isolation
of existence inside a solitary body,
without both of us
ending up in the belly
of some mammoth miscommunication.

We have to be realistic.

Maybe if you go to sleep, I can love you.
Little Concertina,
my hands, fingers and opposable thumbs,
will gather the myriad ellipses of your body into my arms,

and you will be a coddled coiled thing,
notched scales cradled against the smooth skin of my forearms
          and bicep.

Together we make a bundled up swirl of blotch and freckle,
your head,
the weight of your small skull,
tucked against my heart,
both of us murmuring steady vibrations of kinship.

                    And then I will sing to you.
                    And you will not be deaf.

SNAKE

But what will I hear when the song ends?
White noise?
Static?
A bustle of traffic down dirt roads? ATVs ripping the land?
Shots fired for fun on the ranch behind your house by an AK-47?
The poacher's shots? The poacher's daughter bragging
to the ranch manager's daughter in class
about the weekend elk?
The recession's supper?
Or will I hear your own radio?
Blaring the fad you've accepted,
the top forty alternatives to thinking or doing your own composition?
Or perhaps, what will haunt me is just the sound of your voice?
Sound. What is sound? Sound mind? Sound body? Sound effects?

Expectations of answers? Do I have a choice?
Will you scream? Will I?

WOMAN

There is no scream adequate
to encompass both the fear and despair
inherent in our interaction.

We have the potential for misinterpreting intimacy.

If you inject some subcutaneous part of my flesh
with secretions from your glands
—an act of sheer instinct—
I would inevitably end up hurt
or hospitalized
or dead.

Corkscrew Asp, you are the dearth of my imagination.

SNAKE

And you mine.

WOMAN

To see your triangular head,
that closed mouth full of venom,
the diamondback twine of your body...

SNAKE

To see your booted foot,
your open mouth full of half-cocked ideas,
your whole body living the limbic system's legacy of fear and fraught...

WOMAN

Together our mortal terrors are coiled tight and spring-loaded.

SNAKE

We are adrenaline's puppets.

WOMAN

To encounter each other is to empty the universe of history and void
time.

SNAKE

Morning newspaper gotten and forgotten,
the daily catastrophe averted from sight—blight,
your own memories are moot.
Your future is forgotten
or displaced
or fictional.

WOMAN

Armed and legged and necking into position for a better view of
before and **after**,
I glimpse only now.
This is the pistol-loaded standoff with time.

SNAKE

The draw.

WOMAN

Dead heat.

SNAKE

And you,
your full body busted,
are revealed
to be empty-headed.

WOMAN

Dimwitted.

SNAKE

Vapid.

WOMAN

I am every absence known to humans.

SNAKE

The lack of cohort.
The overstuffed abyss.

WOMAN

The missed lunch date three days before the brain tumor is diagnosed
    and the state left for better dying.

And now my own negligent coffin will bury
    every unfinished business and unspoken word.
How frequently I cast aside opportunity in favor of ...

SNAKE

Malarkey.

WOMAN

Yes, petty rages and small-minded temper.
How regularly I relinquish real connection to anything
in favor of sleep...

SNAKE

Or mindless obsession.

WOMAN

I am so tired there is not even regret.
There is this room.
And here, I am my own aspersion because I am blank.

Because I do not know what to do.

SNAKE

"To do or not to do—"
I do
say, "This is not the question."
Your threshold for inactivity is so low
(blow)
I'd almost willingly proffer you this rural hamlet,
let you share my terrain,
as a panacea of passivity.
This Deer Valley,
this cluster of 36 mailboxes
—not all of which correspond to houses—
should remedy your animosity towards inactivity.
But you're still abuzz, abuzz, abuzz—
addicted to being busy instead of just being . . .

You've become a to-do list with tic marks,
a full calendar that doesn't heed the cycles of the moon,
an adroit consumer's shopping catalog,
nothing but a grocery sack of tin cans.
Why do you promulgate solidarity with waste?
After everything we've been through
will you nonetheless waste time,
waste resources,
waste this opportunity to be
intimate
with me?

WOMAN

Bite me.
I am not your rape victim,
your doll-sized handpuppet,
your knock down oak splatter.

(*Snake rattles, mocking*)

And I am **not** the only "being" in this room with susceptibilities.
There is no existence without shades of vulnerability:
living creatures die or are taken down.

Even the lone gunman.
Even the organized terrorist.
The mortal leader of genocide.
Even the lover.

How can a snake be all powerful
if the boyfriend who tried to kill me
couldn't prevent being held up at gunpoint
under a bridge?

Here in my living room I am petitioning the bigger predator.

I call the roadrunner.
I call the king snake.
I call the javalina.
I call the hawk and eagle.

SNAKE

Let there be survival of the fittest—
or survival of the wittiest.
What's another predator in your life?
What's another in mine?

WOMAN

I'm calling my cognitive behavioral therapist.

SNAKE

That's a new one. A twenty-first century talk-show one.
A confessional mesh of grown woman balking
and needing her hand held.
Good luck.

(Snake begins low rattle.)

WOMAN

(To Snake)

Ssssh, it's ringing.

(To Doctor)

I'm sorry to trouble you, Doctor,
but I have a bit of a situation.
Do you have a moment? Yes?
Okay, so I've got a rattlesnake in my living room.

(To Snake)

He's laughing!!?!

SNAKE

(Victory rattle and dance.)

WOMAN

(To Doctor)

So what do I **do**?

(*Wait to hear answer.*)

You want me to sit with my fear?
The emotion is to be feared more than the reality?
"I am my own worst enemy? God, the snake just said that to me.
Well, not in those exact words but really, Doctor,
the snake is talking to me."

(*Wait to hear answer.*)

Of course I can see that my current level of fear sucks
and personally I think my fright so gargantuan
I might hallucinate or pass out
at which point I'd be wholly and completely vulnerable,
so what am I supposed **to do** about the snake?

(*To Snake*)

He's getting his New York Colleagues on the line.
They'll know what to do.
They handled 9/11 and the collapse of the twin towers.
What's a western diamondback
in comparison to hijacked airplanes
and **real** terrorism?

(*To Doctor*)

What's that? They concur?

Just sit with my fear? If you say so.
Thanks for your time, Doctor.

(Click.)

SNAKE

You babbled like Babinski.
Did you get everything all figured out?
Or should I tickle the bottom of your foot?

WOMAN

I'm supposed to just sit with you.
Override my reflexes.
Tolerate your presence.

(Woman turns chair to face stage left and sits directly facing snake. Woman and Snake stare at each other for 30 seconds, long enough for things to become uncomfortable, then Woman gives up, stands, turns chair to face stage front, sits back down, slumped, spent.)

SNAKE

Not too bad.

WOMAN

Good. I did good.

SNAKE

Well, the silent treatment is certainly better than all that hullabaloo about milking.

WOMAN

I suppose so, yes, but I simply wanted us to make antivenom together.

(Contemplative pause.)

How did you come to feel so reviled?
Have humans always looked down on
every underbelly living in quiet submission to the earth?
So what if sometimes you protect yourself.
Who wouldn't? Who shouldn't?
Here, in my living room, there is no hierarchy in my gaze.
You are down and I am out:
                    we are together the makings of equity.

                    Would you prefer this chair?

SNAKE

That would be lovely.

(Snake and Woman switch places.)

WOMAN

Perhaps we have met for some kind of healing.
I think of grief this year,
long nights with the underwater heaving of my lungs.

First assault I lifted my arms skyward
and screamed heavens into hell.
Within a week my body was slaughtered,
disease preying on stress. I'm still ailing.
My left torso is an oak tree,
my heart bust with an ax.

You,
          who wrap around the Rod of Asclepius
          and symbolize all healing,
couldn't you fix me?

SNAKE

I could offer you a mango.
Guava agave passionfruit pomegranate..
Perhaps an apple . . .

WOMAN

Déjà vu. Why not, you Undulating Swell?
I ate the forbidden fruit in Genesis.

You acted on behalf of Satan then,
why would it be different now?

WOMAN

Would you also care for a cherry, you Phallic Tease?

(Snake tongue flicking.)

SNAKE

I can tempt and taunt you so easily.
Why should I desist when you can't resist?
In the beginning was no different.
Desire is a fickle muse,
a ravenous mullable,
contemplation cut short and impulsive,
a catalyst that will always open your eyes
wider than you could have anticipated.
I am here to transform you.

WOMAN

Meddler, you Winkless Wonder, at least for now I can still blink.

SNAKE

How convenient.
Bat an eye, will you?

Neglect to notice anything
you'd prefer not to see?
I can't. Moreover I wouldn't.
My eyes are permanently fixated
on the measure of sky and land
and all that happens therein.

WOMAN

Is that a good thing?
Does witness make you wise?
Does knowledge equate compassion?

What if Eve had been made from one of your ribs instead of one of
Adam's?
Would humanity have turned out more empathetic . . .
or more predatory?

SNAKE

How should I know?
I slither instead of walk on two legs.
However, I do race without arms, race
without trigger fingers—
that's something.
Still, my survival is tenuous, tenacious.

WOMAN

Is this survival? One lifetime?

SNAKE

All our skulls will fall,
our ribs cage dust,
our back bones torque
and torque again.

WOMAN

Charmed Convolution,
    you and I act like we can be intimate
    but our paths split long before the existence
    of an actual snake or an upright human.

Now that we've come together what are we to make
of the usual rung by rung distribution
of mammals going one way, reptiles another?

And where was I in the upper cretaceous?
Crying out? Not crying?
130 million years, or a few decades.
By the time of Lapparentophis defrenni
your spine was already in play:
    a two-vertebrae record going round
    the Saharan desert.

Let Darwin explain why time has been deaf to our pleas,
why my tongue is perpetually too torqued to pray
and yours is forever forked.

SNAKE

The record skips.
The record skips centuries.
The record skips the stories we share with each other.

WOMAN

But you,
Minimalist-without-Limbs-or-Lymph-Nodes-
or-Any-of-the-Gratuitous-Synaptical-Junctures-that-Plague-
Humans-
with-Guilt-and-Regret-and-Fear-and-Indecisiveness,
why do we both resist fossilization?
Or why does geologic history resist us?
Rockabye.
As if what's delicate or fragile,
poor and sick and marginalized,
or merely vulnerable to the elements,
doesn't merit a text in stone.

SNAKE

How did you come to feel so reviled?

Learn to take sadness like some pill,
like encapsulated fate,
like stones plunking to the bottom of your feet.
Let blood run over rock.

I can assure you, the weighted grief,
where you reject histrionics,
does no less justice to sorrow
than rising up against everything in full flail.

I know.

(Snake rises up full flail and rattling.)

Let emotions sink earthward

(Snake sinks, calmed and quieted.)

and acceptance rise up.

WOMAN

Still, My-Myelin Menace,
I'd like—*no quiero mucho*—a small place in history, a footnote,
or better, a place in literature, a single poem,
and for you, the most specialized of all living snakes,
I want to scratch a drawing of you onto red boulder,
line drawing of a front-fanged proteroglyph evolved,
now going pitted and heatsniffing after warmblooded prey at night.

Perhaps to you I represent just another failure
of humans to value the earth and what hugs it.

Today let me be inhuman.

SNAKE

Nice thought. Not possible.

WOMAN

But I am tired of being human.
I really really want to be inhuman.
People are mean.

SNAKE

And snakes are no threat?
We're not really, except to our prey,
or when threatened, shoved, coerced, captured, poked with a stick.

WOMAN

Here, the same as always,
I have chanced upon what you do every night
when sight takes refuge in the unfolding promise
of finding yet another reason to rotate the maxillary bone
and fang something mammalian.

SNAKE

You still think I'm going to bite you?

(*Rattling a little.*)

WOMAN

What am I supposed to think?
Look at the way you wield those unshed ringlets
of dead and interlocked and luminous skin,
rattling—at a woman.

SNAKE

This is what I do.
This is who I am.
No quiero mucho.
I move from the sun to the shade.
One rock here, a patch of soft sand there.
There are only the body's regulations to adhere to.

Be grateful. Be gracious.
Give me space and we'll get along just fine.
I like it here
and won't bite on whim like some newborn rattler . . .
but toy with me, and you'll find fangs so fast sinking into the flesh
            of your thigh
            or wrist
            or calf.

I will sink my teeth down
to the bone of your flippin' tibia . . .

WOMAN

My Ectothermic Foe,
your nostrils are my enemy.
Fierce Friend,
I flush like a target, like the soft thing
you want to sink your teeth into
but taste of me and I will be your mouthful,
your fated swallowing,
the last supper that will ever leave you sated.

SNAKE

Ah, don't get carried away or melodramatic.
Which of us isn't heat-seeking?

WOMAN

I'm not.
Most of the time, when you're not here, I live alone.
I'm a solitary woman.

SNAKE

You're promiscuous.

WOMAN

What do you mean?

SNAKE

How do you think I found this place?
You have a reputation.

WOMAN

What are you talking about? With humans?
They say that about all unmarried women.
But no, not really ... though I confess I took off my shirt
and used it to catch a towhee.
And then there was a hummingbird in a silk blouse.
I caught it hovering between my curtains,
held in my hand, heart beating so small against my lifeline,
and maybe I've caught a head-whipping skink or two,
a blue-tailed lizard, a horned toad and even negotiated a barn swallow
who perched on everything even the bare light bulbs.

And admittedly, you are not my first snake.

SNAKE

I knew it!!!

WOMAN

My first was milk, a snake so fast it went under the baseboard
and back into the wall until I tracked him down
and found him outside my wood-sided shack and caught him,
held him, outside under sky, for a moment.

But really you should know, I barely let people in the house.

SNAKE

Maybe you should open your heart.
Maybe you shouldn't be so standoffish.

WOMAN

Maybe I should call Animal Control.

SNAKE

I'm a reptile.

WOMAN

Only the second definition of "animal" is limited to mammals.
The first merely requires that you're not plantlife,
while the third kind of animal pertains to anything vulgar and brutish.
You are vulgar and brutish. I could call Animal Control.

SNAKE

It's after dusk, they'll be closed. They're not nocturnal!

WOMAN

But I bet they'll have a voice message referring all emergency calls
to the Sheriff's Department and I'll say

"Yes, I know it's a rattler, it rattled at me—and, yes, it's in my
living room"

The dispatch agent might send a deputy who comes
flashing lights and sirens in his striped car.
And on the top of the car could be some two digit number
that he (and I) associate with the strength of his extended family.

And because of his extended family, he might have dealt with this
before,
say in Mountinair or Estancia, a rattler in the house.

SNAKE

What was that phrase your grandmother used to exclaim?

WOMAN

And the deputy has—"Lord Love a Duck..."—yes he does have
that big hefty loop of wire threaded into a pole
so he can lasso your head and keep you at a broomstick's distance

and perhaps because after he comes in you retreat behind the
bookshelf,
he hands me his flashlight, more like a baton, so heavy
I feel the weight drag my arm towards thoughts of brutality,
and then we chase you,
we chase you together for a full thirty minutes,
thirty minutes of a lovely tryst
where I still see only you
but now the diamondback patterns are interspersed
with the lush brown of the deputy's skin,
so smooth I can't look long because I've got to keep my eyes on you,
and he, looking at me, can't look long, cause he's got to keep his eyes
on you
and so he doesn't even notice my breasts or the gun on the wall,
both of which I forgot to properly stash,
because we've got to keep our eyes on you,
and so what happens to vision could be this thing akin to a merger
where your scales are windows onto his flesh
and his flesh windows onto your patterns . . .

SNAKE

Why are you doing this? How could you?
Why would you?

WOMAN

And you, you might be so scared you don't even rattle,
you just press your head down under your body

as if what your spine can do was as vast and encompassing
as the circles in the heaven, 10,000 ellipses,
all the spheres of the heavens rotating at once
into the great vast hiding and dark and begging from behind the
bookcase,
"Don't lift me from the ground by my neck"
and the deputy and I now close as an old married couple
who communicate deft without looking at each other,
saying, "Yes," saying "Got him" saying "Watch out" and saying "Oh
my god"

and then the deputy says "Where do you want him?"

and I might point off the property, and that's where we could let you
go so fast,

and you could go so fast through the grass
to me it looks
as if you never really wanted to spend any time with me in the first
place.

It could, you know, go like that.

SNAKE

Why?
Why would it go like that
when it doesn't have to?

WOMAN

I guess it's not really what I want. I'd prefer it went different.

Even if I'm fair to certain
the deputy would have removed his wrist-cuffed leather gloves
to shake my hand
because that too,
our triangulation with you,
would have been intimate.

But if I took his hand,
it would have been a rebound,
a desperate clutch at *anything*
after everything I feel with you.

The truth is
my hand is wide open and receptive
        to flesh,
        to scale,
        to time,
        to the lines that lead from my head to my heart
        into the future of still being alive
        and not so compromised in my conscience
        that I chopped your head off with a shovel ...

SNAKE

Thanks. Now we're almost parasympathetic.

WOMAN

Decent Fellow, I don't know why I said all that...
Dirt-Encrusted Prairie Saint, we're okay aren't we?

SNAKE

For now.

(Silence, stewing.)

Sprawl!

(Woman sprawls in chair.)

Why did you do that?

WOMAN

You told me to.

(Woman sits up.)

I don't know.
Maybe in lieu of apology.
Maybe because you have some kind of power over me,
some kind of authority that reminds me of other kinds of authority
that happened in my life when I was powerless,
maybe because sometimes I still feel powerless.

Infrared Wheelbarrow, so much depends on
whether or not you strike me.

SNAKE

I was just thinking about sprawl . . .
about the ever-increasing encroachment on my land,
the environment my lineage traversed uninfringed,
and now we've got this hyper-cooperative way of living.

WOMAN

Oh.
Do you think the fact that I'm living out here is sprawl?
What am I supposed to do?
The city is hard on me.
All the lights and noise overstimulate me.
I find peace out here.

SNAKE

You find me out here.

WOMAN

But we're finding a way to coexist, aren't we, My Cat's Eye Gamble?

SNAKE

Perhaps.

WOMAN

Did you hear the one about the wallflower and the walking stick?

SNAKE

Surprisingly, no.

WOMAN

That's us. Wallflower, walking stick.

SNAKE

Is that the punchline?

WOMAN

Yes.

SNAKE

Good one. So which of us is the wallflower? Which walking with a stick?

WOMAN

We could be some joke happening in a bar
because pick-up lines have so many mundane variants.

SNAKE

"Did it hurt?"

WOMAN

"Did what hurt?"

SNAKE

"When you fell from heaven."

WOMAN

"Where have you been all my life?"

SNAKE

"And exactly where do those legs of yours end?"

WOMAN

"You're driving me crazy. All those curves and me with no brakes . . ."

SNAKE

"There are 206 bones in the human body. Want more?"

WOMAN

"Be a broom and sweep me off my feet."

SNAKE

"Shall we fuck like bunnies?"

WOMAN

"You bad bad snake!"

SNAKE

"Have we met before?"

WOMAN

You **do** look familiar.
I have this vague memory of spotting you
after my foot legs and privates
passed over the length of your body in my driveway.
As if our togetherness began not fifty feet from where we are now,
that day last month when my sole missed your sunbaking.
A moment in the driveway we shared in consciousness
only after the fact.
Even that day, the gravel pitched tension under my skin,
if belatedly, rough edged recognition of something primal.

SNAKE

I was no more perceptive or less receptive,
scuttling into brush after you passed

WOMAN

My legs walked the dog on a leash;
my eyes looked toward the wood fence of my courtyard;
my mind pictured the clumped irises secreted away around the corner;
and my heart skipped—*a priori*—
as if peripheral vision registered in my inattentive amygdala.
Somehow I knew enough,
I knew enough to look back.

So here we are.

SNAKE

Again.

WOMAN

What are we going to do, Darling Devourer?

SNAKE

"Frankly my dear, I don't give a damn."

WOMAN

I do give a damn.

SNAKE

So, let there be loco-motion.

WOMAN

Let there be loco-motion?

(This next exchange of lines allows Snake and Woman to get as close as they will ever get. Magnetism is expressed during lines, revulsion between, but the dialogue feverishly decreases the distance between the Woman and Snake until they are separated by mere inches and ultimately embrace, fiercely to close this Act.)

SNAKE

Yes, let us wind through the grasses across the mesa
and up through the boulders to the top of the ridge;
let us keep climbing until I can scale mountains with you,
some red-faced cliff with petroglyphs
or a bluff topped with aspens,
any place we can rise up counterintuitive
while monsoons run down arroyos . . .

WOMAN

As if gravity were always something to succumb to
instead of just another kind of
magnetism

designed to remind you to scale

me

because today my body has become simply some unexpected soft surface
for you to encounter in your environment,
as if love were tactile,
or timely,
as if love didn't have rough edges,
my own elbows and knees,
a scathing surface of jutting collarbone and breast,
together we are a cacophony of softness and hardness.

SNAKE

My spine against your belly.

WOMAN

Your ribs wrapped by the reach of my arms.

SNAKE

My jaw pressed against your sternum.

WOMAN

Hard valley of animal meeting reptile.

SNAKE

The length of our long bodies intertwined . . .

(Embrace begins with the word "intertwined.")

WOMAN

Because I am the one who can help you molt the parts of your body
hardened by parasites, the epidermis solidified so tough
you can't grow or breathe into who you are becoming . . .

SNAKE

(Snake and Woman turn so that Snake faces audience over Woman's shoulder.)

And I am the one who can help you remember
that fear doesn't have to be fraught with expectations of danger;
sometimes it's simply anticipation of interactions not yet
experienced . . .

If there is a reason for our togetherness, let it be vulnerability,
the sloughing off of old ways, the abandonment of fierce exoskeletons
that protect us a little too well,

as if you and I have been calling it safe to be sealed under a bell jar,
as if that vacuum were enough to merit the word "alive"...
when the other option is this...

WOMAN

Intensity of now.

:: Act Three ::
RELEASE

(This Act is about letting go, sensuous and satisfied release, devastation and acceptance, moving towards a separation where fate is forgiven. The act begins with the release of the embrace and reestablishment of distance, as if intimacy were overwhelming and disconcerting, something from which both have to regroup.)

SNAKE

Behind that closed door exists everything you want and everything I want.

WOMAN

No. What we both want is here. What we want is each other.

SNAKE

No I want little nests of little things to swallow.
Baby rabbits and the deer mouse.
Days of digestion.
The vibration of nightlife on my forked tongue.
Tomorrow's sun and a good rock for my cold body.

A nice burrow or found cache of safety.
The occasional slow fuck.

WOMAN

What about me?

SNAKE

You want sky full of sun or stars.
Days of connection, nights of solitude.
Calls to your mother, pictures of your nephew, coffee with friends.
The dirt path shared with cows and coyotes.
The chance to poke through bear scat and discern prickly pear.
A good home restored to safety.
The occasional slow fuck.

WOMAN

What about you?
What if I want you?
What if I don't want this to end?

SNAKE

"Want" and "need" are two different things.
We each have our own fates to embrace,
our own lives to try to do justice to.

WOMAN

But you're the one who said **being** is more important than **doing**.
Why, My Favorite Unrequited, can't we at least just keep being?
Here, in the intensity of now.

SNAKE

Because I'm a snake.
Because you're a woman.

WOMAN

Are you sure you're not just a Skitty Kitty?

SNAKE

Meow.

WOMAN

That's not fair.

SNAKE

Shucks.

WOMAN

You with your Scales,
    Do you honestly think you know anything about justice?
    About balancing this and that,
    the old garden's old stories of good and evil,
    the way every day is these same old choices from Eden,
    the same burden of knowledge . . .
                        and temptation.

Is your life simple or do you also pit perturbation against balm?
Do you have to weigh fear against desire and decide which will triumph?
My life is complex. My life is sad.

SNAKE

What hooey!

WOMAN

Okay but this is sad.
My Familiar Serpent, you're about to abandon me.

SNAKE

No, not really.
We might never have met.
Sometimes less is more.
Less is what we should covet.

WOMAN

True enough.
Even abandon can be wanton,
the way you shed your whole skin under the lilac bush,
as if the act of discarding
were simply another kind of blossoming.
Let there be such blossoming.
Let there be the appropriate parting of the flesh.
Abandon can leave behind fear,
can relinquish regret,
can offer freedom,
some strange liberation so primal the body is reclaimed, even reborn
perhaps.

So let me dump
ditch
desert
discard
dispose of
throw out *everything* . . .

SNAKE

All the better to keep
and remember
and hold
and clutch
and cleave to the minutes we share.

WOMAN

So this is it.

SNAKE

And this is good.

WOMAN

Enough.

SNAKE

Your house is a heart.
You are heart.
My lungs are breathing the length of your body into my being.
Dispassionate doesn't suit me; distance does.
So let the heart beat and the mitral valve open to the universe we
know as living.

WOMAN

Pit Viper,
This crepuscule with you pales
next to predators with malice.
If you bite me, I will assume this:
We did not know how to negotiate the door.

Here goes.

Let the mitral valve open to the universe we know as loving.

(*Woman opens symbolic door.*)

SNAKE

Loving, leaving, loving cleaving,
snakeweed, cholla, prickly pear.
land, light, sky, sand
We are in this together.

WOMAN

Even in the exodus?
Even when the sky pours out of a hole in the ozone?
Even when ice melts one place and flows a mile thick over Ohio?
Even when the earth shakes and shakes until we all tremble?
When I curl up alone in my bed every night?
During continental drift?
As land masses shift and carry us apart and carry us together
and we leave our homelands,
        your Africa,
        my childhood,
        your kin—the cobra, the asp, the black mamba,
        my kin—the bitten ones.
Both of our bodies constellations of stars in the night sky on a
cloudless night.

SNAKE

Yes.

WOMAN

Yes.

SNAKE

Yes.

WOMAN

Heavens heartbeating, earthbound dreaming.
Right now your mouth is merely some plush wetland
while mine is a red land mass overcome with already longing
for the earth to turn
to spin
to bring us back round to each other.
My mouth is overcome.

Umuhle.

SNAKE

You are beautiful to me.

WOMAN

Ukamhlaba

SNAKE

You are of the world.

WOMAN

Hamba ne tinyoga ntima.
Hamba ne tinyoni.
Hamba ne umgankla.

SNAKE

Go with the black snakes.
Go with the birds.
Go with the kudu.

WOMAN

Hamba nge sibhakabhaka.
Hamba kanye umhlaba.

SNAKE

Go by way of the sky and go with the land.

WOMAN

Ngiya kukhulula wena.

SNAKE

I release you.

(Snake sets down his rattle, quietly, and Woman picks up shed rattle.)

WOMAN

Hamba,
Go!!!

(Snake begins exit.)

na sala
. . . and stay

(Snake looks back.)

kahle
well.

(Snake leaves completely. When he's gone, Woman shakes rattle.)

Ngiya kutsandza wena.

(*Lights, curtain.*)

Acknowledgments

First I would like to thank the prairie rattlesnake who graciously visited my home and heart. I would also like to send warm-hearted gratitude to that particular snake's literal and metaphorical kin: *the catalysts for transformation must be thanked.*

On a less metaphysical but equally vital level, I would like to thank Suzanne Sbarge, Rhiannon Mercer, Francesca Searer, and Barbara Geary at 516 ARTS for their invaluable support. Gratitude also goes to Skye Pratt who grew up in Swaziland and who (over coffee in Albuquerque, New Mexico) both translated a poem I'd written in English into siSwati and then patiently tutored me on how to make the sounds. Thanks to Mitch Rayes for loaning sound equipment for pre-show recordings (and teaching me how to use it).

I also appreciate the support of KUNM 89.9FM and Women's Focus Host Carol Boss, plus Elaine Avila, Bob Holman, Simon Ortiz, Kris Mills, Rudolfo Serna, Hue Walker, Bradley's Books, and th3 *e1emental orke5tra*, who composed music for the book release's after-party. Hearty thanks to Tricklock Theater company members, in particular, Elsa Menéndez and Kevin R. Elder for their advice and support. And of course, I would be bereft if I didn't thank the Moriarty Sheriff's Deputy who helped me out and my Cognitive Behavioral Therapist who did—yes—receive a frantic rattle-informed phone call.

I also want to thank Wayne Gudmundson and Suzanne Kelley from New Rivers Press.

Here I extend gratitude to the National Endowment for the Arts for the Fellowship in Poetry, as well as to McCune Charitable Foundation who provided support at a critical juncture during a hard-pressed time, and to the New Mexico Literary Arts for their unexpected kindness.

And I will always remain indebted to both JB Bryan (who designed this book and published my first book, *Red as a Lotus*) and Alan Davis (who will publish this book and also published *Mortar & Pestle*). Without the faith of these two editors from La Alameda Press and New Rivers Press respectively, I would have no literary career at all.

And finally, very special thanks go to artist Travis J. Farnsworth for his vital feedback, support, suggestions, and encouragement during a brief but critical juncture in my writing process. One of his sculptures even inspired the poem that alludes to an Ezra Pound quote—the one with the Botticelli imagery. Also I was really pleased to have his rendering of the Minoan Snake Goddess on the cover.

Thanks everyone!

Lisa Gill is the recipient of a National Endowment for the Arts Fellowship in Literature and a New Mexico Literary Arts Gratitude Award. She is the author of the poetry collections *Red as a Lotus*, *Mortar & Pestle*, and *Dark Enough*. A graphic memoir titled *Caput Nili: How I Won the War & Lost My Taste for Oranges* is also forthcoming and includes art by Kris Mills. Recent publications include *Tuesday; An Art Project, 1913; A Journal of Forms; The Bigger Boat* and also a poem in the National Endowment for the Arts' Annual Report. She served as artistic director of *STIR: A Festival of Words* and received her MFA with distinction in creative nonfiction from the University of New Mexico. She has performed widely from the Taos Poetry Circus to the Thom McGrath Visiting Writers Series in Minnesota and the Seattle Poetry Festival. She favors collaborations and has worked with visual artists Kris Mills, Becky Holtzman, Suzanne Sbarge, Valerie Roybal, Heidi Pollard plus video guru Bryan Konefsky and Dome Artist Hue Walker. She has performed with countless musicians including Mike Balistreri, Mark Weaver, Janet Feder, J.A. Deane, C.K. Barlow,Mitch Rayes, Kurt Heyl, The Michael Vlatkovich Trio and th3 eιemental orke5tra. She has now moved to Albuquerque, though *The Relenting* was written while living rural near Moriarty, New Mexico.

Photograph: *Wes Naman*

New Rivers Press (NRP) was founded in 1968 by C. W. "Bill" Truesdale and has published more than 330 titles. In 2001, after Truesdale's death, the press, located in Minneapolis, went into suspension. Alan Davis, an author and editor with the press, and Wayne Gudmundson, a photographer with book production experience, both professors at Minnesota State University Moorhead (MSUM), revived and relocated NRP to MSUM as a teaching press. Its dual mission is to publish the best work of every character that it can find, especially literature by new and emerging writers, and provide learning opportunities for students, who can earn a Certificate in Publishing. The press honors Truesdale's progressive spirit by publishing work with a strong sense of place that speaks to our troubled times with *satyagraha* (the truthforce), empathy, and aesthetic courage. For more information, visit our web site at http://www.newriverspress.com